Igor Stravinsky

THE RITE OF SPRING

IN FULL SCORE

Dover Publications, Inc., New York

This Dover edition, first published in 1989, is a republication of the edition originally published by Izdatel'stvo "Muzyka" (State Music Publishing House), Moscow, 1965. The Russian-language Foreword and the Russian portions of the list of instruments have been newly translated. The French section headings have been moved from the music pages to the new table of contents and replaced on the music pages by English equivalents of the Russian headings.

The publisher is grateful to the Paddock Music Library, Department of Music, Dartmouth College, Hanover, New Hampshire, for the loan of the score.

Manufactured in the United States of America
Dover Publications, Inc., 31 East 2nd Street, Mineola, N.Y. 11501

Library of Congress Cataloging-in-Publication Data

Stravinsky, Igor, 1882–1971.
  [Vesna svi͡ashchennai͡a]
  The rite of spring.

  Ballet.
  Reprint. Originally published: Vesna svi͡ashchennai͡a. Moskva : Izdatel'stvo "Muzyka", 1965.
  Duration: 33:00.
  I. Title.
M1520.S9V47 1989   88-753344
ISBN 0-486-25857-2

THE RITE OF SPRING

(literally, Holy Spring)
Scenes of Pagan Rus' [Russia] in Two Parts
by Igor Stravinsky and Nicolay Roerich

The original Russian headings appear on the corresponding music pages. The English renderings of them given here reflect Stravinsky's own mature preferences. A few renderings that differ, but have been hallowed by usage, are supplied in square brackets. (At the end of this table of contents is an attempt at a different kind of translation.) The French versions of the titles, added here in italics, are taken from the original score.

NOTE: As a curiosity that may possibly be of some use to researchers, the following represents a novel (perhaps foolhardy) attempt to translate the original Russian headings into recognizable English, but also literally (as if each component Russian word really had a meaning of its own): "THE KISS BESTOWED UPON THE EARTH," "Introduction," "Springtime Soothsayings: Dance of the Fashionable Girls [or Women]," "The Simulated Abduction," "Vernal Round Dances," "The Game of the Two Towns [or Walled Settlements]," "The Procession of the Eldest-Wisest [Man]," "The Kiss Bestowed Upon the Earth (the Eldest-Wisest)," "The Figured Dance in Honor of the Earth [or The Acquisition of the Earth Through Dancing]," "THE GREAT SACRIFICE," "Mysterious Games of the Girls: Movement in Circles," "The Honoring of the Chosen One [female]," "The Appeal to the Forefathers," "The Ritual Performance of the Elders as the Forefathers of Mankind," "The Great Sacred Dance (the Chosen One)."

FOREWORD

by Boris Mikhailovich Yarustovsky
(1911–1978)

The Rite of Spring belongs to that class of artistic productions which, in their significance, come close to being creative manifestos. In this composition by Igor Stravinsky, despite its serious inner contradictions, there emerges in many ways a new system of musical language. The universe of its musical thoughts and the principles of their development are highly original. By its unusual stylistic audacity, the score of *The Rite* has exerted an intense and widespread influence on the entire musical culture of our era. Almost all twentieth-century composers, even those in disagreement with the conceptual basis of the work, have paid attention to it and have been inspired by it to a greater or lesser degree.

The "Scenes of Pagan Rus'," as the composer called them, were created in the era before the storm, on the immediate threshold of the first imperialist war, in the "neighborhood" of such works as Scriabin's *Prométhée*, Rachmaninoff's *The Bells*, Strauss's *Elektra*, Bartók's *Bluebeard's Castle*, Ravel's *Daphnis and Chloe*, Mahler's Tenth Symphony and Schoenberg's *Pierrot Lunaire*.

Of course, these works and their subjects are quite diverse, and each of them reflects its composer's originality and individuality. Nevertheless, in the methods of their musical language there is a common element, connected with the social atmosphere of the time: the premonition of approaching cataclysms and upheavals of society; an intensification and occasionally even a violence of feeling, and at the same time an alarming expectation of something frightening and unknown. For Russian art in that prerevolutionary era the most characteristic theme was

Scythianism. It appears in works of literature (Blok, Gorodetsky), music (Prokofiev's suite) and painting (Roerich). Frequently the figure of the ancient Scyth was associated in the circles of the artistic intelligentsia of that time with the form of the coming giant, of the full elemental force that would bring with it a new, unusual, but frightening and perhaps dangerous beginning.

In order to convey this range of emotions, new expressive means were called for, intense and expressionistic. In these same years new currents of prewar bourgeois art appear; some of them, the most extreme, were given remarkable names, such as Fauvism [the art of wild beasts]. (Close to them in Russian literature were the Acmeists, to some degree the Futurists, etc.) The taste was for rough primitivism, ultra-originality, heightened emotions, exotic landscape and vigorous dance—just a few hallmarks of those currents. Sharp contours, stark coloring, intense and odd rhythms, harsh contrasts—these were characteristic signs of that artistic style.

That was the atmosphere in which *The Rite of Spring* was created as well. Its first contours, in the composer's words, flashed into his mind as early as those days in 1910 when he was completing *The Firebird:* ". . . there arose a picture of a sacred pagan ritual: the wise elders are seated in a circle and are observing the dance before death of the girl whom they are offering as a sacrifice to the god of Spring in order to gain his benevolence. This became the subject of *The Rite of Spring*" [from *Chroniques de ma vie*]. As early as the beginning of summer, the newspaper *Russkoe slovo* (July 15, 1910) reported that "the academician N. K. Roerich; the young composer of *The Firebird*, I. F. Stravinsky, and the choreographer M. M. Fokine are working on a ballet called *The Exalted Sacrifice*, based on ancient Slavic religious customs." It was no accident that the composer turned to the well-known artist and ethnographer Roerich: No one, perhaps, had a better knowledge of the daily life and mores of the ancient Slavs; as an artist he gained a feeling for them in his own field of visual imagery. But the composition of *The Rite* began later—in the year 1912 and 1913. By that time the initial idea for the ballet had changed considerably. Its original name was now applied to the second part only. The choreographer Fokine was busy with other productions, especially Ravel's ballet, and was replaced by the famous dancer Nijinsky. In the period between the conception of *The Rite* and its composition, Stravinsky had managed to write another ballet, one of his best works—*Petrushka*.

The Rite of Spring was produced at the Théâtre des Champs-Elysées in Paris by the ballet troupe of the famous Russian impresario Diaghilev. (The composer worked with him from the time of his first ballet, *The Firebird*, until Diaghilev's death in 1929.) The first performance took place on May 23, 1913. It was an unusually riotous occasion: members of the audience whistled, stamped their feet and honked auto horns. The curtain was dropped in mid-scene. The composer was distressed and fled the theater in awful confusion: "I knew the music so well and it was so dear to me that I couldn't understand why people were protesting against it prematurely without even hearing it through" [from the magazine *Amerika*, no. 76, 1963, p. 26].

It must be said that even later the stage history of the ballet proved to be unenviable. Thus, when presented in 1921 by Massine (again with Diaghilev as impresario), the ballet failed once more to gain laurels for its composer. But barely a year after the scandalous world premiere—in April 1914—the music of *The Rite*, performed as an orchestral suite at the Casino de Paris under the direction of Pierre Monteux, had elicited a rapturous reaction from the audience. Within a brief time it conquered all the major concert platforms of the world.

How can such a strange phenomenon be explained? Possibly the ballet has not yet found a choreographer with sufficient insight into it; its lack of success in the theater may also be ascribed to its lack of plot, since it consists merely of a suite of thirteen different scenes depicting the life and nature of the ancient Slavs. But the chief reason for the thorny theatrical path of *The Rite of Spring* clearly lies elsewhere: the novelty of its music, its complex world of sound, imperiously demanded the concentrated, undivided attention of the listeners for the full transmittal of its thought and the perception of the purely musical essence of the work. The scenic and choreographic images distracted the listeners from the new and unfamiliar sound configurations.

The heroes of "the springtime sacrifice" are the people of pagan Rus', strongly tied to the earth, to the elemental forces of nature and its yearly cycle, people prompted by the primitive but persistent forces of human nature, the instincts of prolongation of life and preservation of the tribe. The pantheistic essence of *The Rite* has been expressed with sufficient clarity by the composer himself: "In *The Rite of Spring*," he wrote, "I wished to express the bright reawakening of nature, which is restored to new life—a full, spontaneous reawakening, a reawakening of universal [maternal] conception" [from "What I Wished to Express in *The Rite of Spring*," *Muzyka*, no. 14, 1913]. The composer was able to give form to this process of the birth and growth of the life forces with enormous artistic power, and to make it possible for the listener to feel the very atmosphere of the springtime visions; and—this is very important—he carried this out primarily on the basis of Russian song material.

To some extent, no doubt, the scenes of vernal renewal, of the growth of elemental forces, had various points of correspondence with the emotional atmosphere of prewar and prerevolutionary Russia. In this respect Stravinsky proved to be a great national artist of his day. But at the same time, the work gave distinct indications of how limited its outlook on the world was—for example, in the development of its human characters, in the destiny of the young forces active in the work. By bringing them into contact with the stern principle of ritualism, with the implacability of the wise elders, by emphatically depicting the unchangeable cycle of the birth, growth and death of living forces as something eternally predetermined—as man's fate—Stravinsky demonstrates with sufficient clarity all the inner contradictions and limitations of his philosophy of life.

The way in which this process is reflected as Russian "Scythianism," as the actions of a barbarically primitive, uncivilized mob, not hesitating to achieve its goals through cruelty and murder, is thoroughly typical of his perception of the world.

In these "Scenes of Pagan Rus'" there are thirteen episodes (lasting from one to five minutes each) grouped in two parts, seven in the first part ("A Kiss of the Earth") and six in the second ("The Exalted Sacrifice"). In the first part of the ballet (and corre-

y in the music of the orchestral suite) the
s presented with scenes of springtime games
ned by girls and youths. After the Introduc-
-a unique "morning symphony" depicting
ire awakened by the springtime sun—"The Au-
rs of Spring" and "Dances of the Young Girls"
present the first groups of girls and youths, who
seem to tease and entice each other with the sunny,
springlike freshness of life's renewal. The third episode, "Ritual of Abduction," marks the first appearance of the manly, impulsive principle: the selec-
tion and "kidnapping" of a girl. The fourth episode,
"Spring Rounds," brings us back to the contrasted
movements of male and female round dances and
their intermingling.

In "Ritual of the Two Rival Tribes" the fiercely
active principle appears again: duels between
youths, rough skirmishes between rival clans. After
"The Kiss of the Earth" (which follows "Procession
of the Oldest and Wisest One"), the climax is the
furious "Dancing Out of the Earth"; in this scene for
the full company, all the immense energy of the life
forces, finally freed from wintry bondage, seems to
spurt forth.

The second part of the suite, "The Exalted Sacrifice," also begins with a scene of nature: in the half-
light of dawn, in the tensely watchful silence, the
youths renew their games. This is followed by the
"Mystic Circle of the Young Girls." With a light,
"snaky" motion they encircle the Doomed One—
the girl destined to be the offering to the god of
Spring. In "The Naming and Honoring of the
Chosen One" the crowd surrounds the immobile
victim and praises her.

The next two episodes, "Evocation of the Ancestors" and "Ritual Action of the Ancestors," open
up a different world to us, gloomy and harsh. The
old men have come here merely to participate in the
spring performance. They "shamanize," preparing
for the frightful act of expiation. The Chosen One
begins her final dance. When she is weary and
seemingly just about to fall on the ground, the old
men, stealing up, do not allow her to make contact
with the earth and thus save herself, but instead lift
her up to the sky. The Bacchic, ritualistic "Sacrificial
Dance" forms the end of the second part and of the
work as a whole.

The large-scale symphonic cycle of *The Rite* is a
monumental suite, a series of group dance scenes
(essentially, there is only one solo dance) developing, so to speak, in the form of two grandiose,
dynamic growth-sequences that emerge suc-
cessively. In the first part, dynamic focal points are
provided by the men's scenes, "Ritual of Abduction" and "Ritual of the Two Rival Tribes," and by

the final full-company scene, "The Dancing Out of
the Earth." The dynamic summits of the second part
are "The Naming and Honoring of the Chosen
One" and "The Sacrificial Dance."

The musical language of *The Rite* consists of three
compositional strands that are individualized with
sufficient clarity. The girls' scenes are lyrical, with
the melodic principle predominant. The youths'
scenes are boisterous and explosive, with the element of rhythm clearly to the fore. Finally, there is
the mysterious, severe world of the elders, with the
harmonic archaism peculiar to it and its ominous,
"dark" timbres and measured rhythms. The interac-
tion of these three strands is also the musical basis of
the work's dramatic structure. The contrast and in-
terpenetration of the first two strands is the basis for
the development of the first part; the conflict between the first two strands and the third is the foun-
dation of the symphonic drama of "The Exalted
Sacrifice" and especially its concluding "Sacrificial
Dance."

"Lord! how happy I will be when I hear this
performed!" Stravinsky wrote in one of his letters
while composing *The Rite* [letter to A. N. Rimsky-
Korsakov written at Clarens, 1912, preserved in the
MS Dept. of the Leningrad Institute for Theater,
Music and Film, Section B, Division VIII, No. 532].
It was as if twenty years, and not merely two, had
passed since the writing of *The Firebird*. Yes, the
composer was right: the distance in time separating
his first and third ballets, the difference in their
musical language, truly seemed gigantic. In *The Rite*
Stravinsky found new musical means of expression,
new ways of employing those means, a new develop-
mental logic. In a brief essay it is difficult to expound
the essence of these innovations, but in their general
lines they consist of the following.

In his music the composer operates primarily with
laconic sound formulas, three- and four-note
motives. Stravinsky derived many of these from old
Russian chants, such as the so-called calendrical
Slavic songs. In the "girl" episodes such as "Spring
Rounds" and "Mystic Circle of the Young Girls,"
their presence is especially notable. They are also
connected with folk-music conceptions by the principle of their development: repetition with vari-
ations. Nevertheless, by departing frequently from
the principles of folk composition, Stravinsky intro-
duces something entirely new in the way he uses and
develops these motives. Perhaps the most notewor-
thy element in this respect is, first of all, his inexhaustible inventiveness in metrical and rhythmic
variation of the motives: their extremely diverse
shifts "to the right" and "to the left" along the
horizontal, their displacement from strong to weak

parts of the measure (that is, the alteration of the metrical quality of each tone), the introduction of changing meters or, as the composer himself called them, "meters subjected to the principle of variation," variation at the level of the musical measure. In a few episodes the meter changes almost with every measure (3/4, 5/4, 7/4, 11/4). Secondly, the novelty resides in the creation of the most diverse superimpositions of one melodic line over another, with the most intensive use of ostinato methods—in the construction of multilevel sound complexes (the closing episode of each part). Connected with this is a phenomenon that might be called a dissonant "flickering" or "vibration." Supported by an ostinato bass formula that constantly recurs in "rotation," one or the other of the melodic motives is "contaminated," so to speak, by the tones of its lower "neighbor." As a result, the initially simple, unpretentious folk-tune motive suddenly begins to "flicker" and "vibrate"; each of its elements, diatonic tones, becomes "complex," so to speak, radiating dissonant secondary tones. Often such superimpositions have a polytonal character; that is, the lines superimposed on one another are in different keys. For example, this can be heard even in the Introduction, when an F-major motive in the oboe is superimposed on an ostinato G-major phrase of the alto flute. Frequently the composer combines motives in keys that are different but share the same third (F major and F-sharp minor in "Ritual of the Two Rival Tribes," F-sharp major and G minor in "Ritual of Abduction").

All this expands the sphere of dissonance, and the dissonance often ceases to be a harmonic "weak spot," becoming instead a habitual element in a dynamically enriched serial tone row. Also connected with this is the abundant use of chord clusters with secondary levels of complex tone combinations. Analogously to the harmony, in his rhythm as well Stravinsky shows his dynamic side above all. Frequent examples of polyrhythm, of contrast between evenness of rhythmic pulsation and unevenness of rhythmic accents, of the unperiodic structure of metrically changing passages, are to be found in all the "men's" episodes of The Rite. In these same episodes the powerful sonority of the orchestra, heightened by sharply accented "chord-blots" and by the complication of the rhythmic groupings, suddenly gives way to resolute unisons or frequently to rhythmic passages for solo percussion instruments. The gigantic crescendo of sonority in the final episode of each part is staggering in its masterly increase in sound "pressure" while maintaining a precise feeling for form and logicality of structure.

Stravinsky's imagination is also inexhaustible in the art of musical linking. There is great diversity in the fusions of the folksong motives and oddly linked phrases, including some whose endings vary and are truncated at different points. Thanks to the intensity of the inner life of the motive, the composer has the option of repeating it a great number of times.

Stravinsky makes extensive use of a curious method of "sprouting" motives, the "birth" of a motive from the tonal outline of those preceding it. Thus, for example, the mournful theme of "Spring Rounds," which first appeared in the tonal atmosphere of "The Augurs of Spring," is later transformed in "Mystic Circle of the Young Girls," while the theme of "Procession of the Oldest and Wisest One" has its origin in the preceding episode, "Ritual of the Two Rival Tribes." There are quite a few examples of this migration of motives. All of this cements the musical development, "symphonizes" the score and allows the composer to introduce organically even other methods of musical connection: thematic "influxes" and connective musical arches. In general the rondo principle, which manifests itself in an unusual number of guises, is practically the most characteristic formal element in The Rite, even though the episodes themselves, as a rule, are in open order and not rounded off.

Perhaps Stravinsky's preeminent talent manifested itself with special force in the orchestration of The Rite. Dramatization and characterization by means of timbre played such a great role that, essentially, in analyzing the work it is necessary to speak of developing timbre-motives. Frequently the composer consciously chooses characteristic motives in direct connection with the peculiarities of a given instrument: its nature, the sonorities of its registers, its range and other features. To each instrument playing solo the composer almost always assigns its own thematic element. In The Rite, timbre is the most important constructive factor of the whole work. Stravinsky's handling of the instruments of the orchestra is new and unique: his accented chords in the strings often sound percussive, while the actual percussion is really inexhaustible in its expressive function, for example in the final episode of the suite. The role of the woodwinds elicits special attention, because of both their unusual number (five of each) and the inclusion of seldom used instruments. Unusual color is provided by low woodwind registers (flutes in the Introduction, English horn in "Ritual Action of the Ancestors") or by seldom used "small" instruments (the small clarinet, the trumpet in D in "Procession of the Oldest and Wisest One"). The richness of timbre in the score of The Rite testifies to the truly creative revelations of its composer—an authentic magician of the modern orchestra.

The Rite of Spring is a complex and contradictory work. It is an innovative composition in the true sense of the word, opening new artistic horizons in the development of modern music. And at the same time these "Scenes of Pagan Rus'" engendered a passion for all sorts of "barbarities," images of primitive savagery, intentional harmonic hardness; they established a basis for unrestrained experimentation in the area of atonal sound combinations.

New, urban rhythms are reflected in *The Rite*, the new outlook on the world on the part of the dwellers in the modern capitalist city, with its heightened nervous susceptibility, intense inner life and sharpened perception of the evil principle. The various innovations of the composer's musical language—especially in the area of the "emancipation" of rhythm, the integrated application of polytonal thinking, the creation of multilevel sound complexes and of a new, intensive relation to folk material—have exerted enormous influence on the musical culture of the twentieth century. There is no doubt that even Soviet composers, while rejecting many aspects of the conceptual basis of *The Rite of Spring*, while reinterpreting and surmounting a great deal of it, have nevertheless not remained indifferent to its music. It has been a stimulus not only toward a more dynamic use of meter and rhythm, but also toward a broadening of the harmonic system and certainly toward the enrichment of dramatization by means of timbre.

A pupil of Rimsky-Korsakov's national school, Stravinsky proved to be one of the masters of modern Western art, but his esthetic principles are extremely alien to our socialist culture. All the same, the best compositions of this indubitably outstanding artist of our time, who was associated for many years with the traditions of Russian professional and folk creativity, are deserving of our attention and study.

The appearance of *The Rite of Spring* on the desktops of our composers can by no means be considered as a simple accident. It is striking and instructive in many ways.

INSTRUMENTATION

Piccolo
3 Flauti (Fl. III = Picc. II)
Flauto contralto (G)
4 Oboi (Ob. IV = C. ingl. II)
Corno inglese
Clarinetto piccolo (D, Es)
3 Clarinetti (B, A) (Cl. II = Cl. b. II)
Clarinetto basso (B) (= Cl. IV)
4 Fagotti (Fag. IV = C-fag. II)
Contrafagotto

8 Corni (F) (Cor. VII, VIII = Tube tenori B)
Tromba piccola (D)
4 Trombe (C) (Tr-ba IV = Tromba bassa Es)
3 Tromboni
2 Tube

Timpani piccoli
Timpani grandi
Triangolo
Tamburino
Guero (rape)
Cimbali Antici (As, B)
Piatti
Gran cassa
Tam-tam

Violini I
Violini II
Viole
Violoncelli
Contrabassi

Piccolo
3 Flutes (Fl. III = Picc. II)
Alto Flute (G)
4 Oboes (Ob. IV = Eng. Hn. II)
English Horn
Small Clarinet (D, E♭)
3 Clarinets (B♭, A) (Cl. II = Bass Cl. II)
Bass Clarinet (B♭) (= Cl. IV)
4 Bassoons (Bsn. IV = C-bsn. II)
Contrabassoon

8 Horns (F) (Hns. VII, VIII = B♭ Tenor [Wagner] Tubas)
Trumpet in D
4 Trumpets (C) (Tpt. IV = E♭ Bass Tpt.)
3 Trombones
2 Tubas

Small Timpani
Large Timpani
Triangle
Tambourine
Guiro
Antique Cymbals (A♭, B♭)
Cymbals
Bass Drum
Tam-tam

Violins I
Violins II
Violas
Cellos
Basses

With a view to the varied capabilities of different orchestras, each of the two Timpani parts has been made independent. But it is understood that each note will be performed by one player only, except for the passages in which both are specifically designated. The simplest grouping calls for 5 Timpani: Timpano Piccolo (high B), 2 Small Timpani (E♭ and D) and 2 Large Timpani (B♭ and G), on which two performers play simultaneously. When the second performer is not occupied, he can help the first performer with tuning, so that the latter can continue playing. But if there is a greater number of instruments available, they can be separated into two distinct groups, and the two performers will easily distribute the notes between them.

At number 39, combine two measures into one, analogously to the indication at number 41 (9/8 = 4/8 + 5/8) by regarding the first barline of the measure as a dotted one.

Playing time 33 minutes.

ЧАСТЬ ПЕРВАЯ
ПОЦЕЛУЙ ЗЕМЛИ
Вступление

FIRST PART
A KISS OF THE EARTH
Introduction

ВЕСЕННИЯ ГАДАНИЯ
ПЛЯСКИ ЩЕГОЛИХ

THE AUGURS OF SPRING
DANCES OF THE YOUNG GIRLS

30
Picc.
Fl.
Fl. c-a.
(G)
Ob.
C. ingl.
C. ingl. II = Ob. IV
Cl. picc.
(Es)
Cl.(B)
Cl. b.
Fag.
Fag. IV = C-fag. II
Cor.
Tr-be
(C)
Tr-ni
Timp.
Tr-lo
C. Ant.
V-ni I
div. in 2
p sub. e stacc.
V-ni II
p sub.
pizz.
sul G
V-le
div. in 3
4 sole
tutte altre
3 V-c. soli
V-c. altri
C-b.
p sub.

33
Picc.
Fl.
Flatterz. 7
I
II
sempre sim.
Fl. c-a. (G)
Ob.
C. ingl.
stacc.
Cl. picc. (D)
(Flatterzunge)
Flatterzunge
Cl. (B)
Cl. b.
(Flatterzunge)
Fag.
I. II a2
III
sim. sempre
C-fag.
Cor.
I. II. III. IV
Tr-ba picc. (D)
Tr-be (C)
Tube
V-ni I div.
V-ni II
V-le
V-c. div.
pizz.
C-b.

ИГРА УМЫКАНИЯ   RITUAL OF ABDUCTION

43
Picc.
Fl.
a2
Fl. c-a. (G)
Ob.
III
C. ingl.
Cl. picc. (Es)
I
II
III
Cl. (B)
Fag.
Cor.
Tr-ba picc. (D)
Tr-be (C)
Tr-ni
43
4 V-ni soli
V-ni I
div.
unis.
V-ni II
div. arco
arco
unis.
V-le div.
pizz.
arco
arco
V-c.
arco

ВЕШНИЕ ХОРОВОДЫ

SPRING ROUNDS

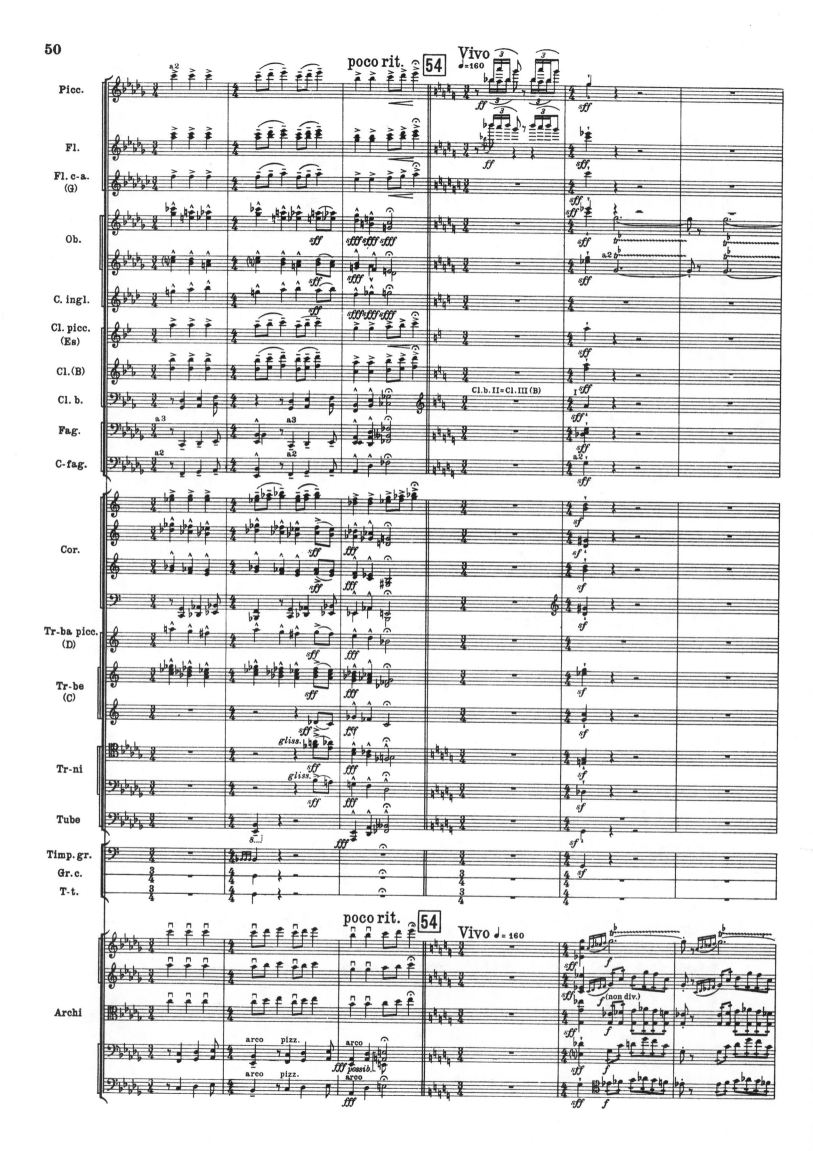

ШЕСТВИЕ СТАРЕЙШЕГО-МУДРЕЙШЕГО

PROCESSION OF THE OLDEST AND WISEST ONE

ПОЦЕЛУЙ ЗЕМЛИ
(Старейший - Мудрейший)
THE KISS OF THE EARTH
(The Oldest and Wisest One)

ВЫПЛЯСЫВАНИЕ ЗЕМЛИ
THE DANCING OUT OF THE EARTH

ЧАСТЬ ВТОРАЯ
ВЕЛИКАЯ ЖЕРТВА
Вступление

SECOND PART
THE EXALTED SACRIFICE
Introduction

ТАЙНЫЕ ИГРЫ ДЕВУШЕК
ХОЖДЕНИЕ ПО КРУГАМ

MYSTIC CIRCLE OF
THE YOUNG GIRLS

*) быстро скользнуть палочкой треугольника, образуя дугу на поверхности инструмента.

*) Run the triangle beater quickly over the instrument's surface, drawing an arc.

ВЕЛИЧАНИЕ ИЗБРАННОЙ

THE NAMING AND HONORING
OF THE CHOSEN ONE

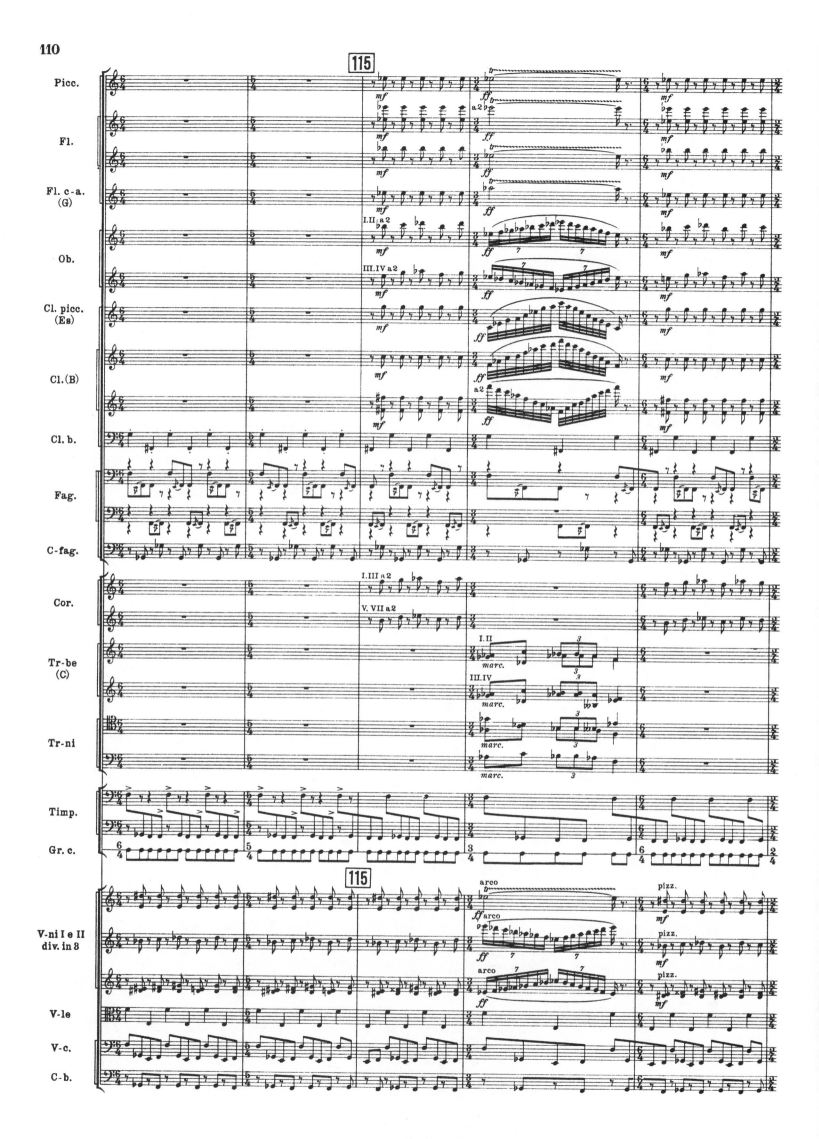

ВЗЫВАНИЕ К ПРАОТЦАМ   EVOCATION OF THE ANCESTORS

ДЕЙСТВО СТАРЦЕВ-ЧЕЛОВЕЧЬИХ ПРАОТЦЕВ

RITUAL ACTION OF THE ANCESTORS

ВЕЛИКАЯ СВЯЩЕННАЯ ПЛЯСКА
Избранница

SACRIFICIAL DANCE
(The Chosen One)

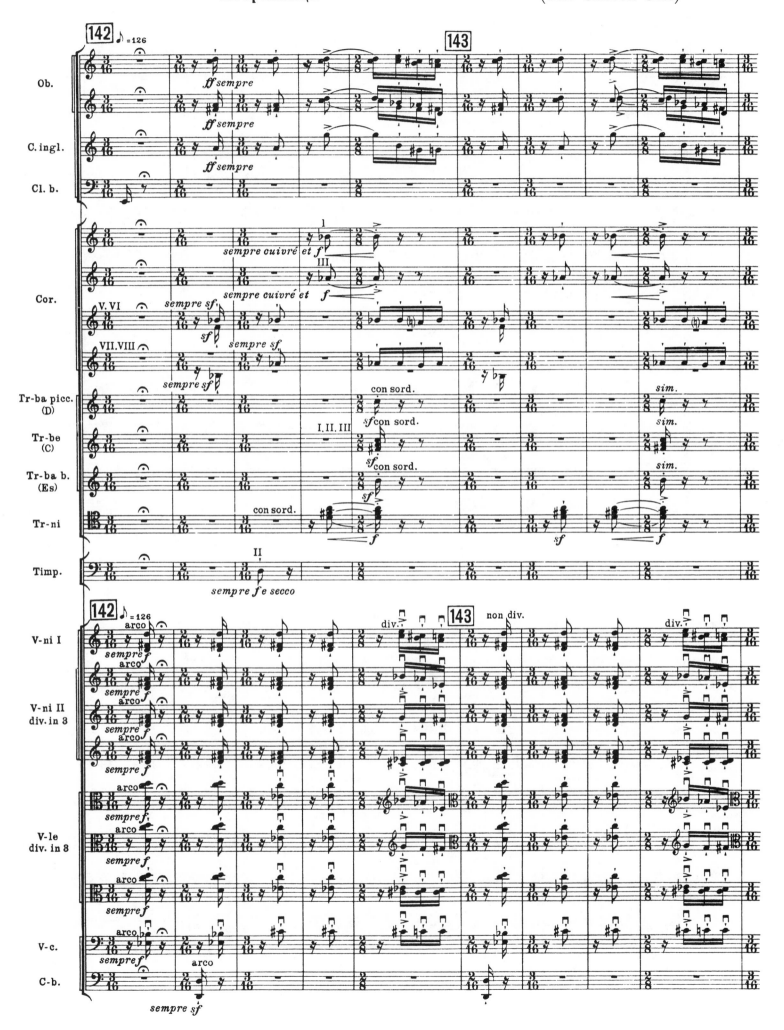

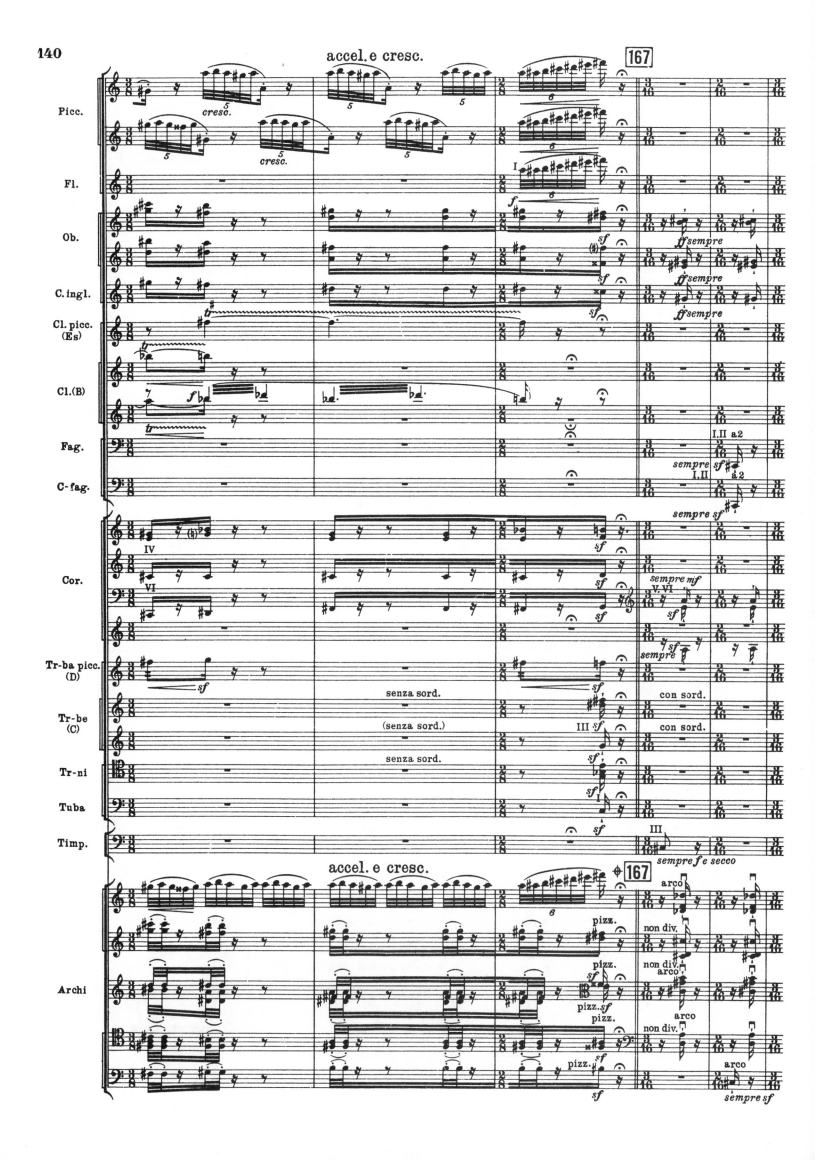

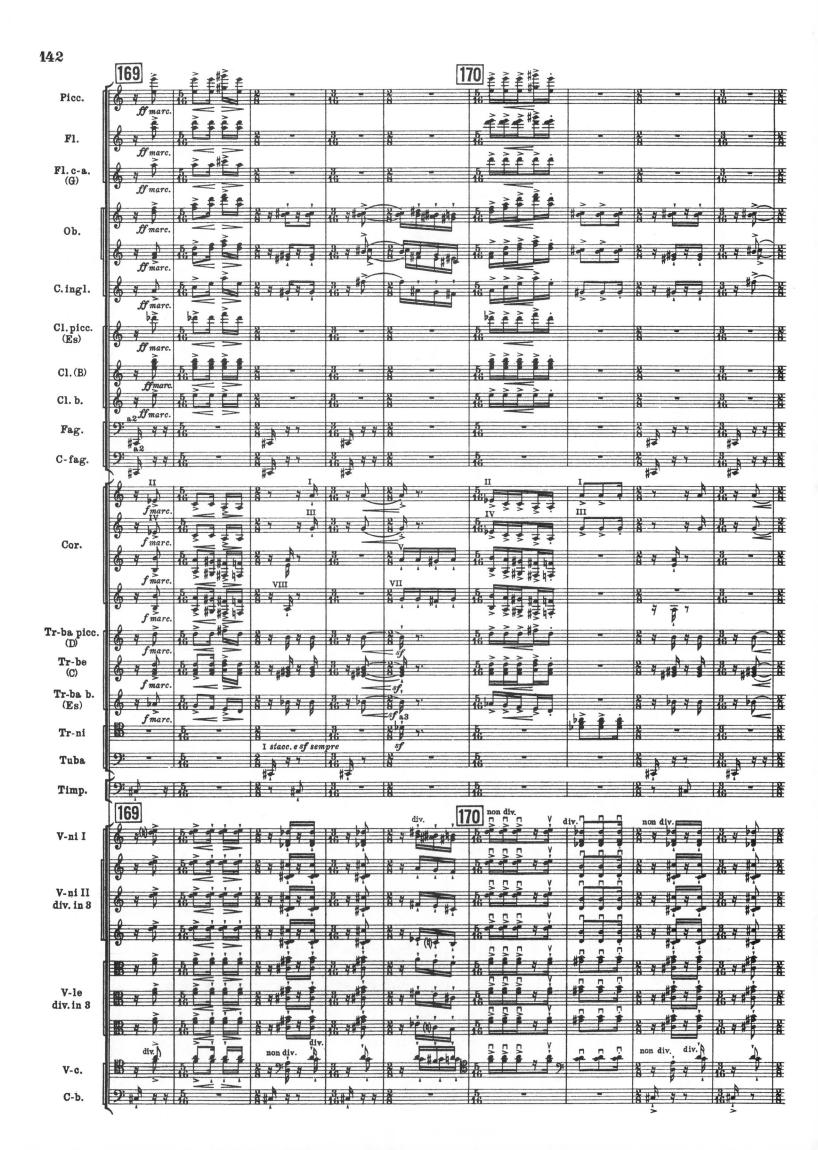

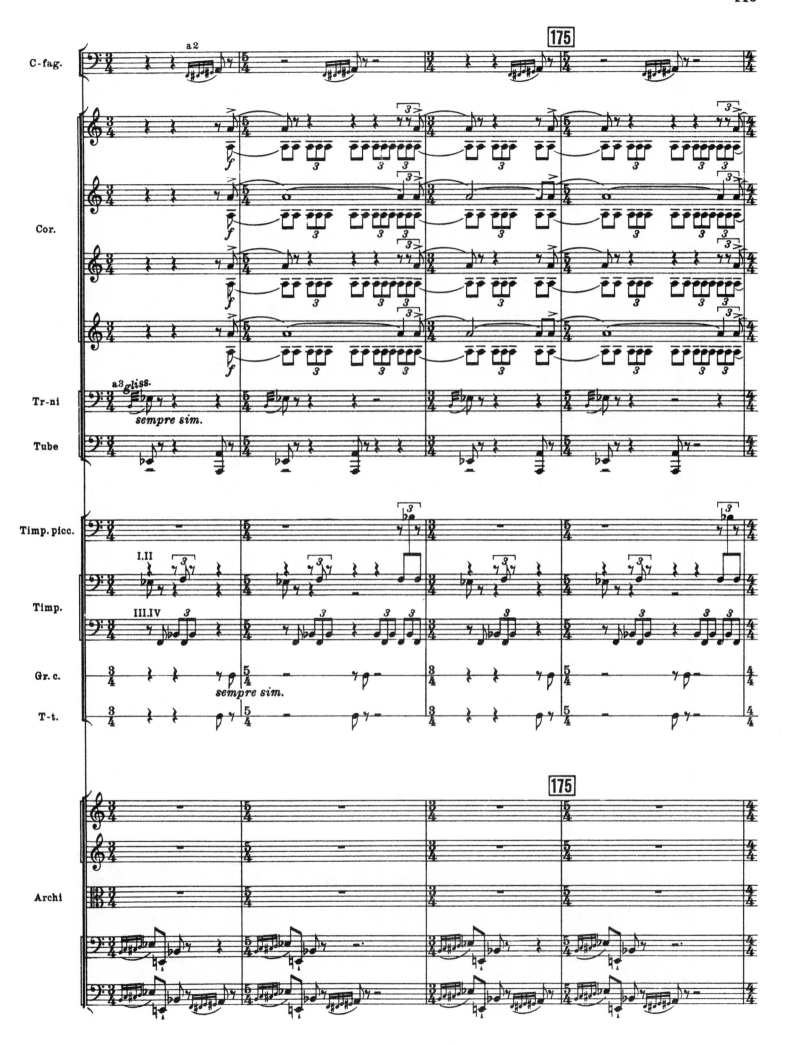

152

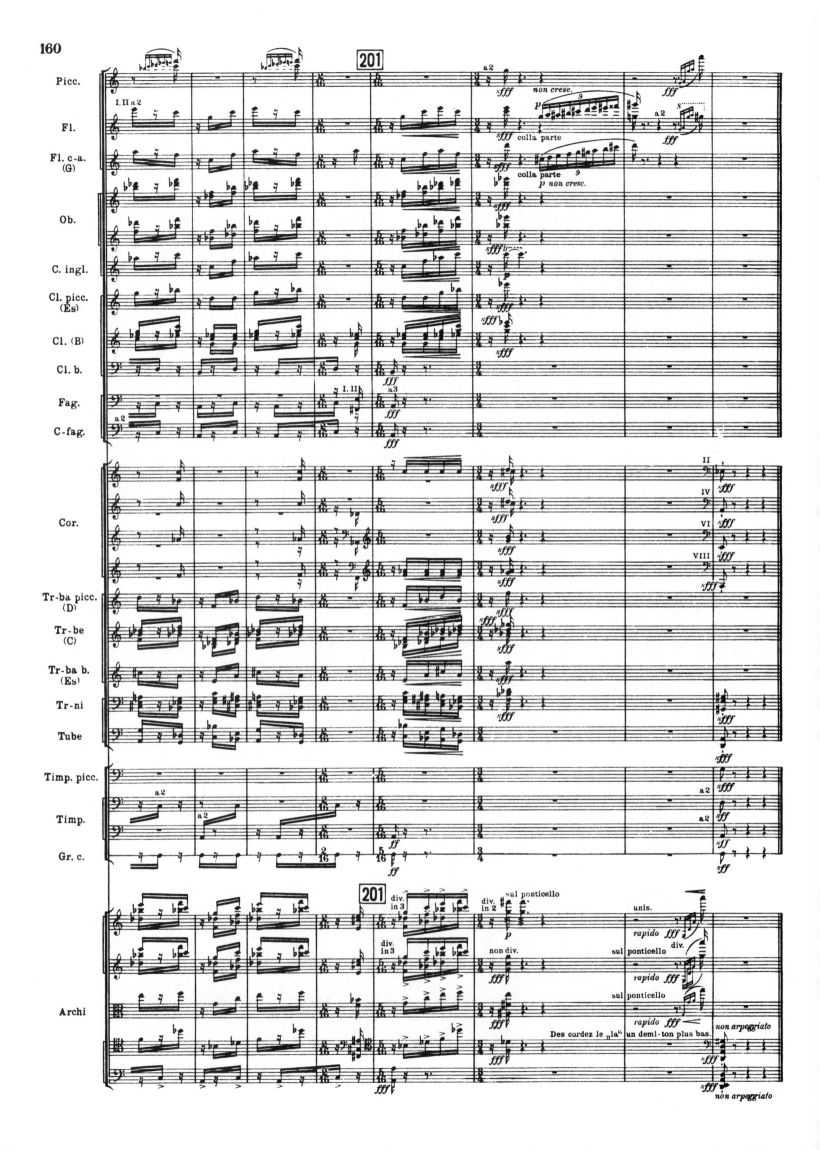